BLUEGRASS STANDARDS

16 SONGS ARRANGED
FOR SOLO GUITAR IN "TRAVIS PICKING" STYLE

ISBN 978-1-4234-0624-2

HAL•LEONARD®
CORPORATION

7777 W. BLUEMOUND RD. P.O. BOX 13819 MILWAUKEE, WI 53213

Visit Hal Leonard Online at
www.halleonard.com

Ballad of Jed Clampett

from the Television Series THE BEVERLY HILLBILLIES

Words and Music by Paul Henning

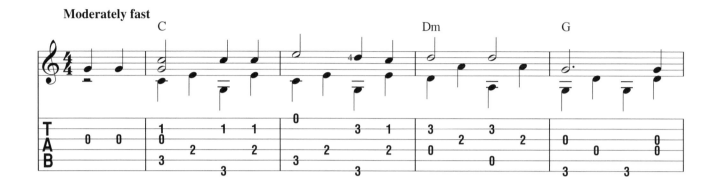

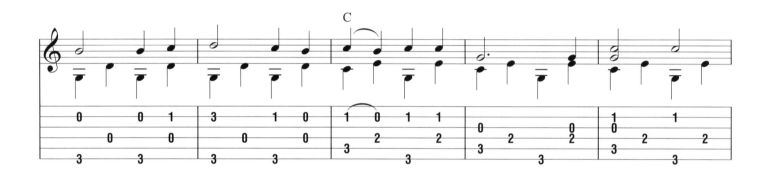

*T = Thumb on 6th string

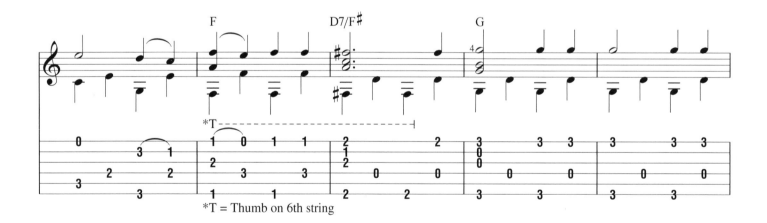

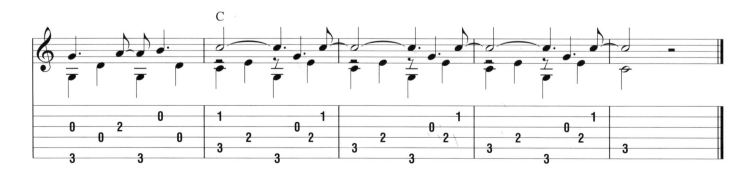

Don't Get Above Your Raising

Words and Music by Lester Flatt and Earl Scruggs

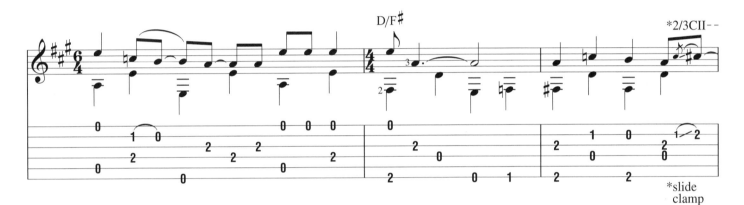

*slide
clamp

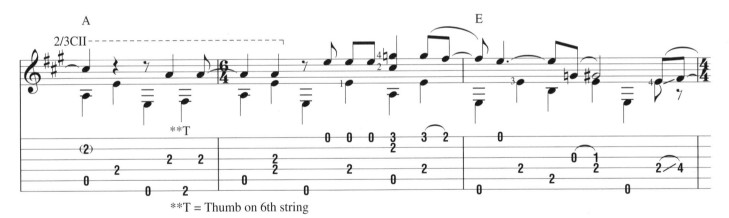

**T = Thumb on 6th string

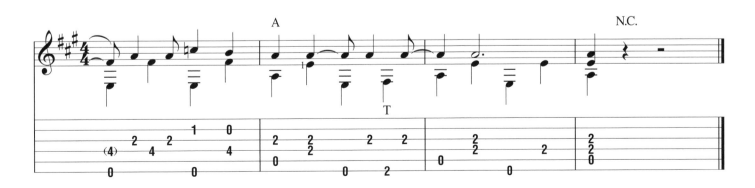

Blue Ridge Cabin Home

Words and Music by Louise Certain and Gladys Stacey

*T = Thumb on 6th string

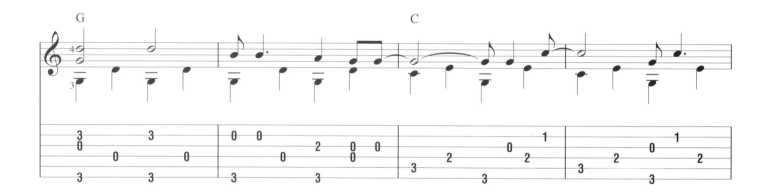

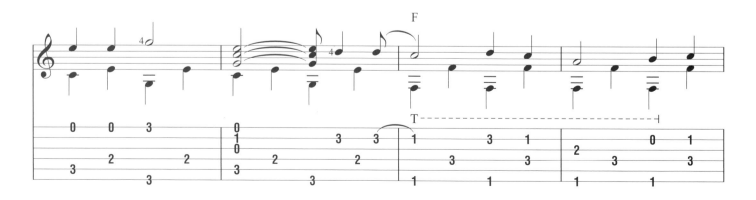

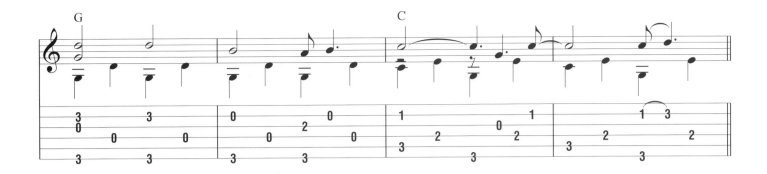

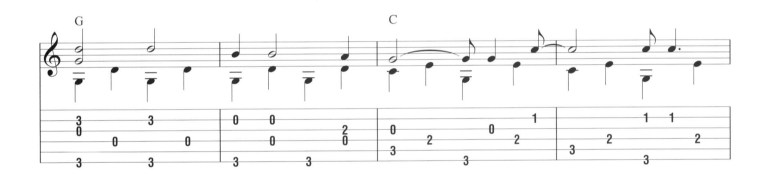

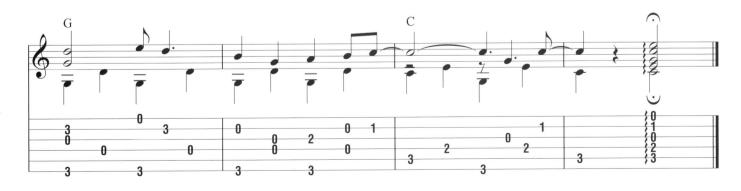

Blue Yodel No. 4
(California Blues)

Words and Music by Jimmie Rodgers

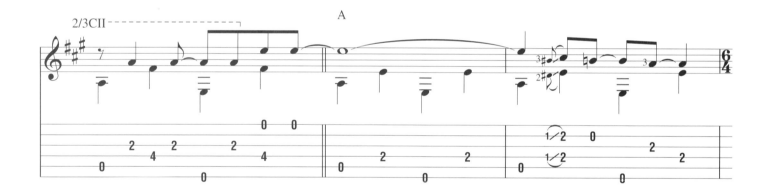

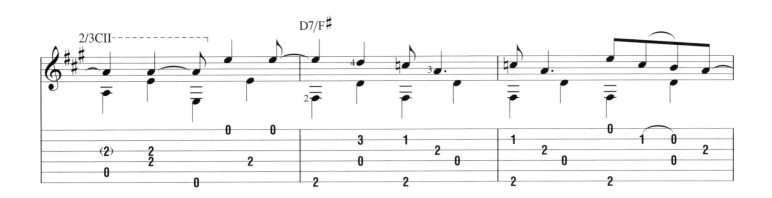

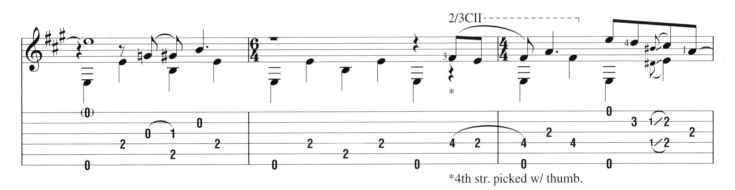

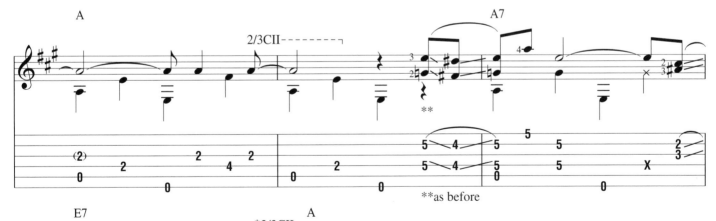

*4th str. picked w/ thumb.

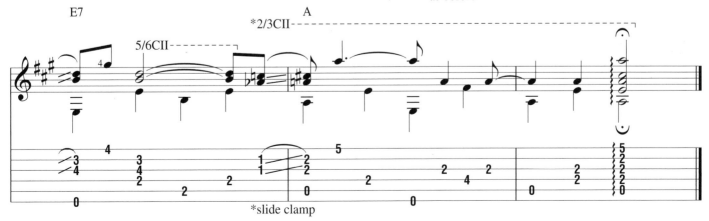

**as before

*slide clamp

Can't You Hear Me Calling

Words and Music by Bill Monroe

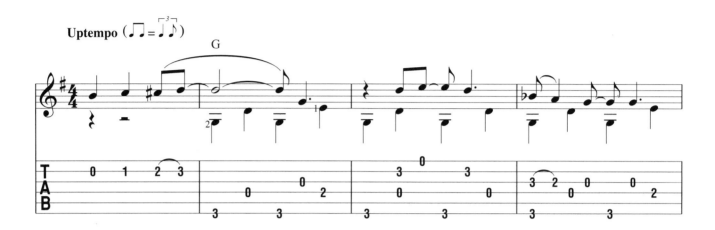

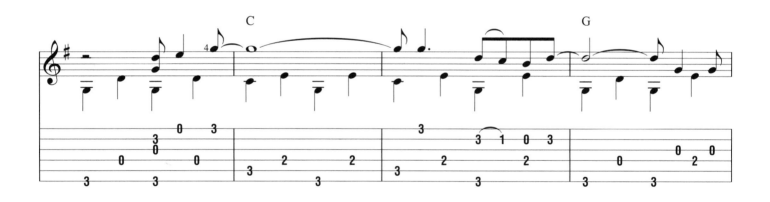

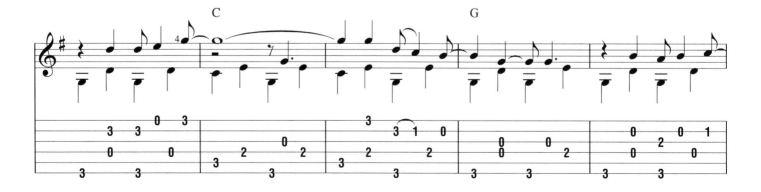

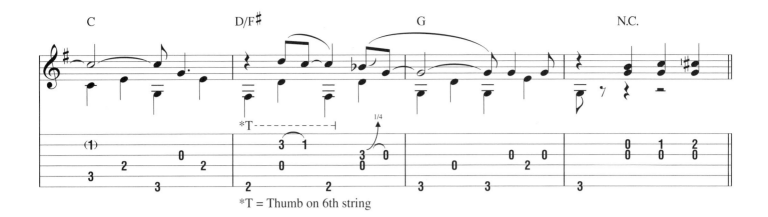

*T = Thumb on 6th string

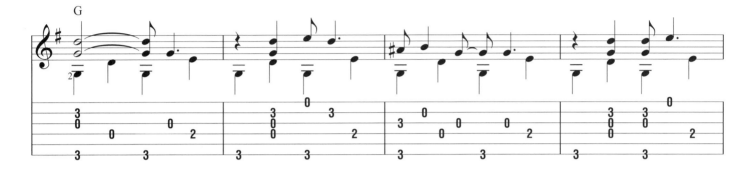

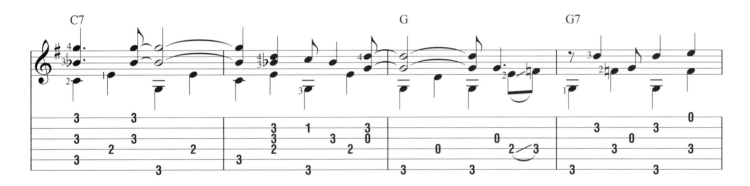

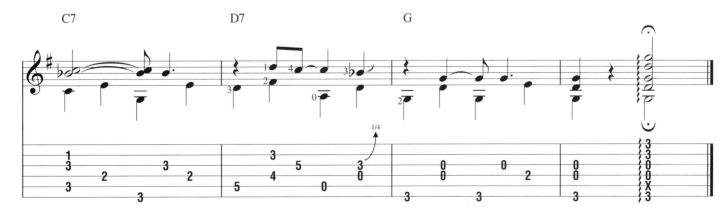

Dark Hollow
Words and Music by Bill Browning

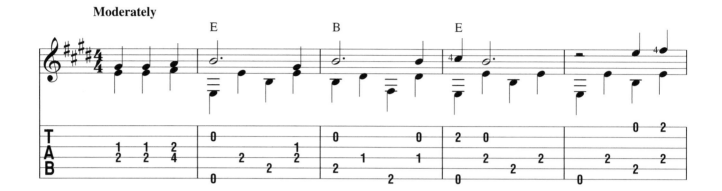

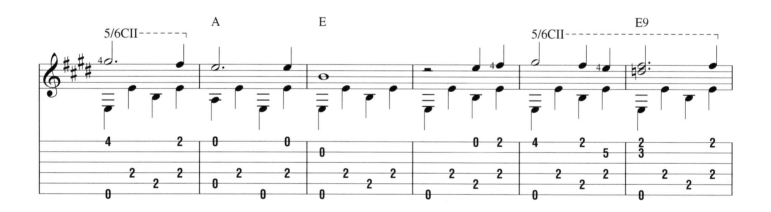

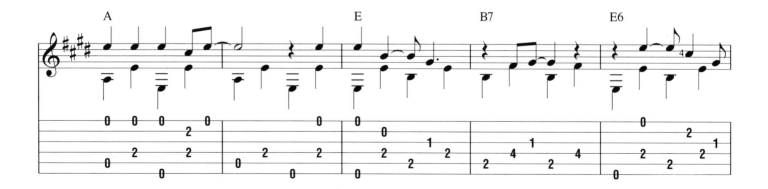

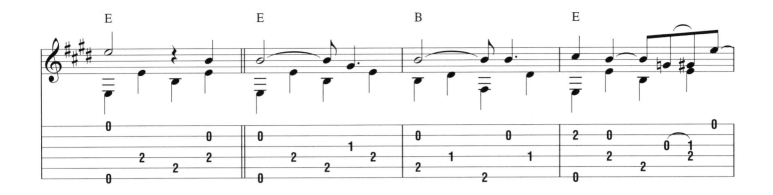

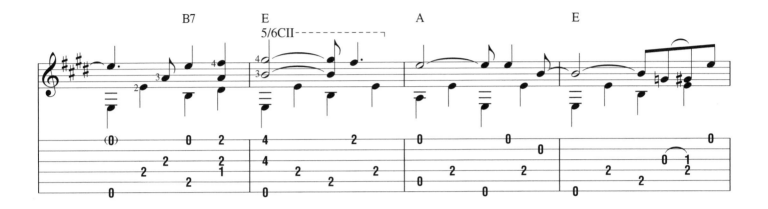

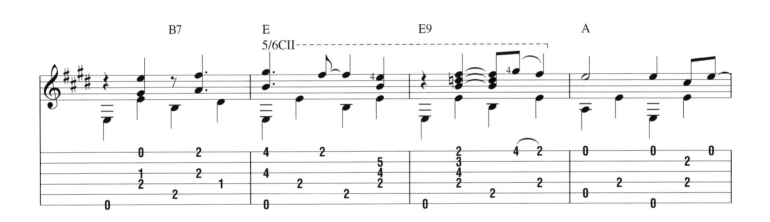

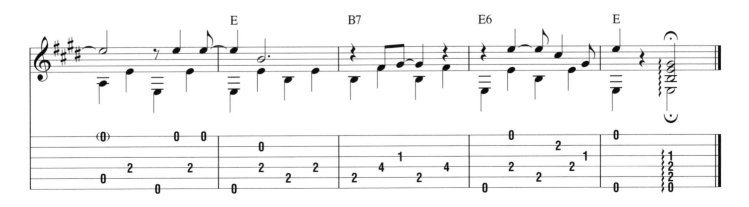

Doin' My Time

Words and Music by Jimmie Skinner

Drop D tuning:
(low to high) D-A-D-G-B-E

Moderately

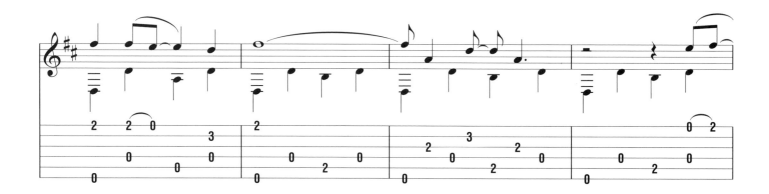

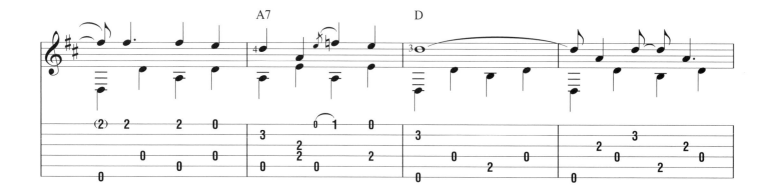

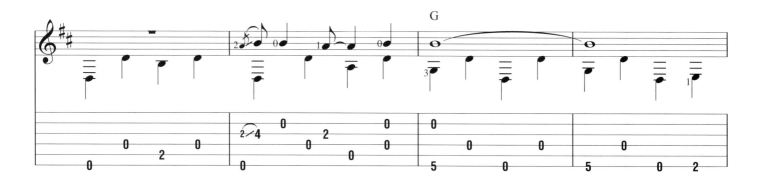

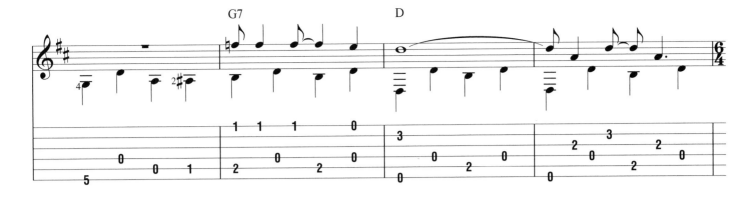

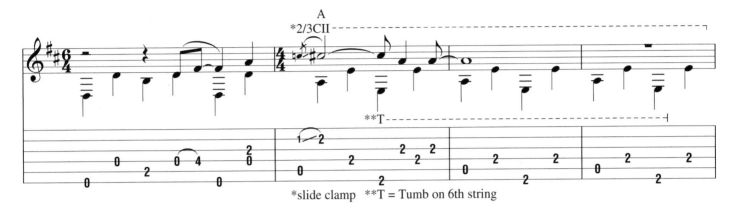

*slide clamp **T = Tumb on 6th string

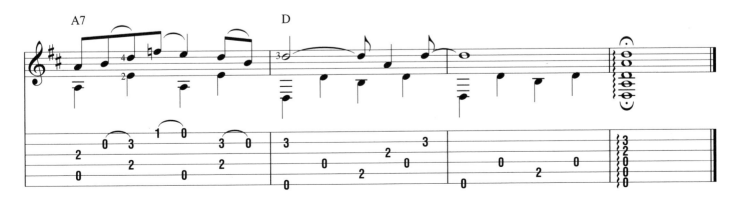

I'll Go Stepping Too

Words and Music by Tom James and Jerry Organ

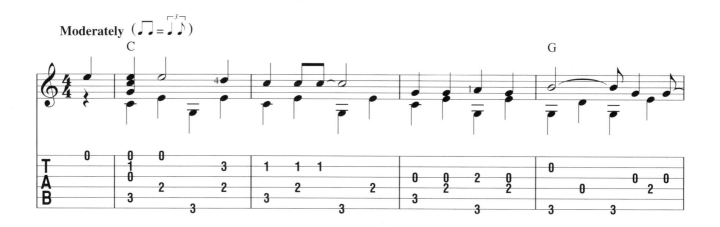

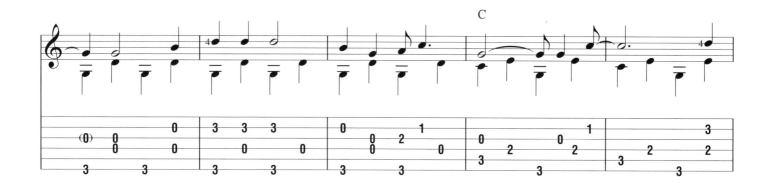

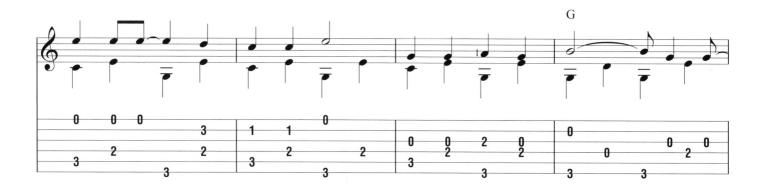

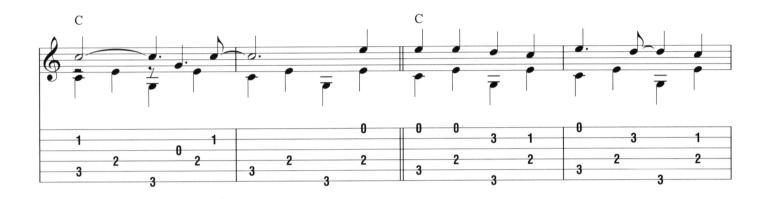

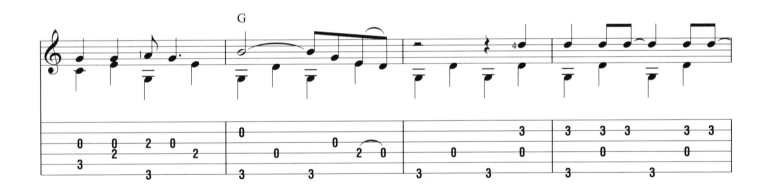

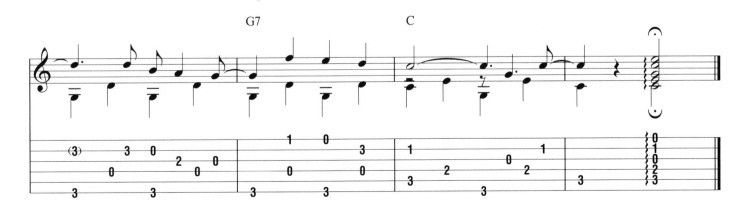

I'll Never Shed Another Tear

Words and Music by Lester Flatt

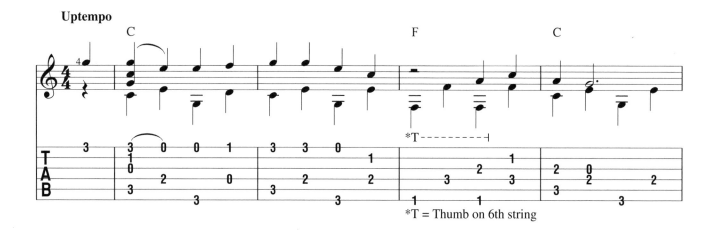

*T = Thumb on 6th string

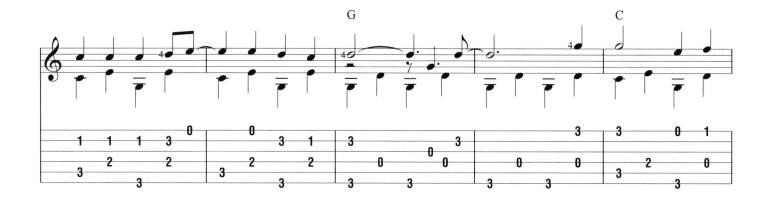

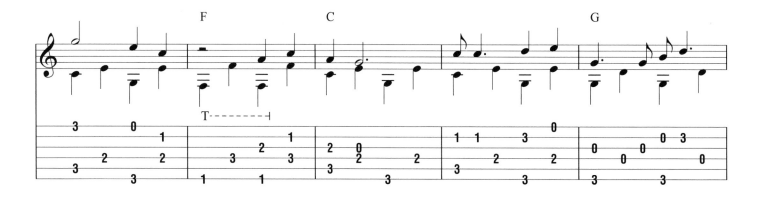

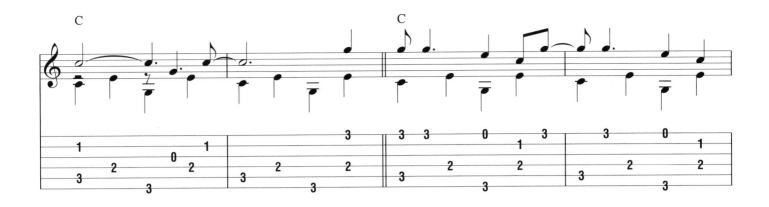

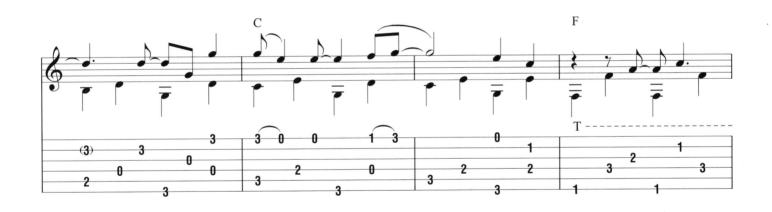

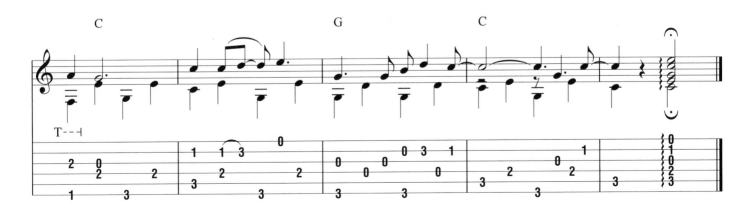

I'm Goin' Back to Old Kentucky

Words and Music by Bill Monroe

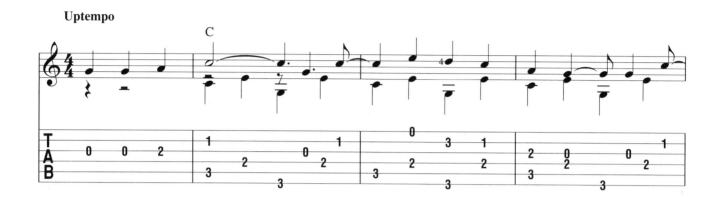

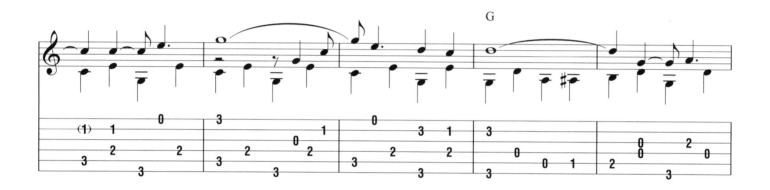

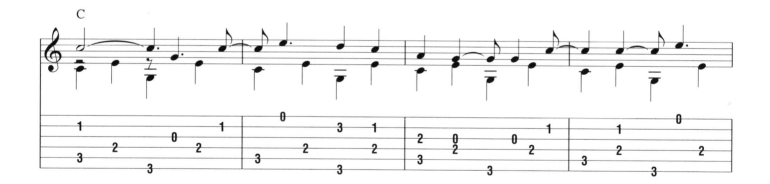

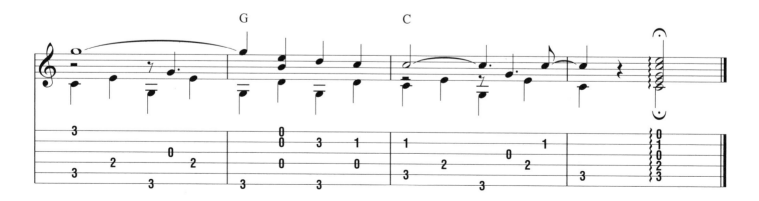

We'll Meet Again Sweetheart

Words and Music by Lester Flatt and Earl Scruggs

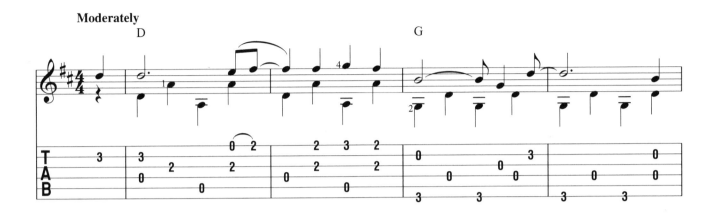

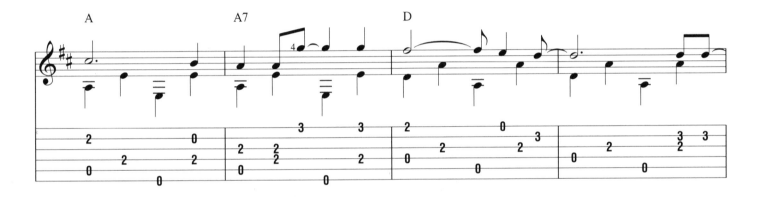

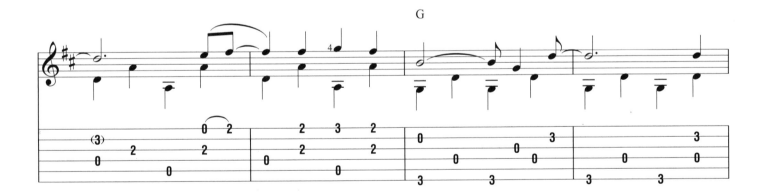

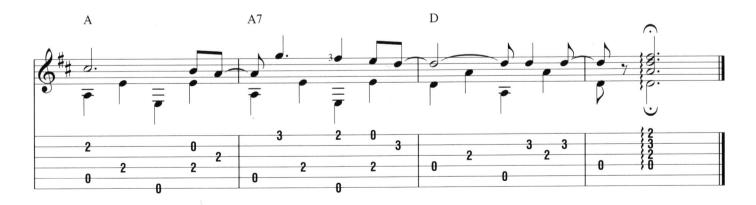

If That's the Way You Feel

Words and Music by Ralph Stanley and Peggy Bland

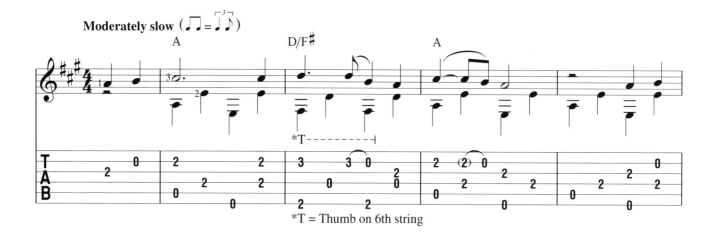

*T = Thumb on 6th string

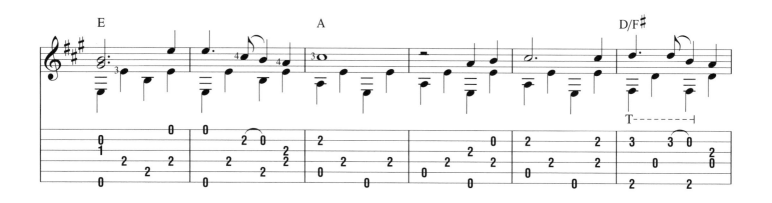

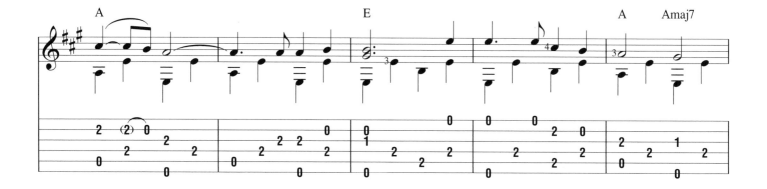

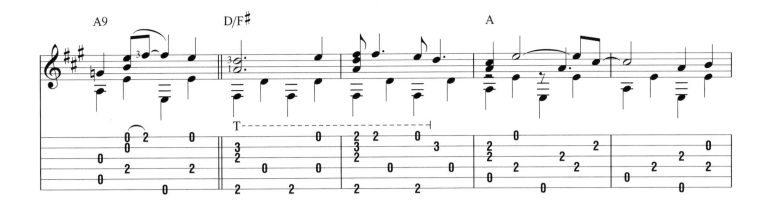

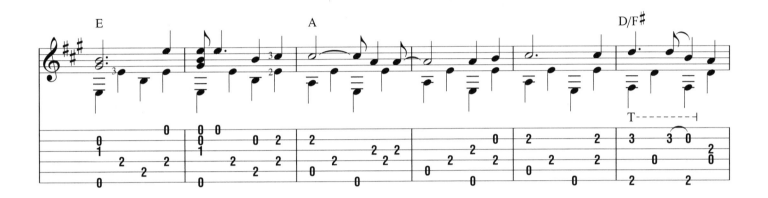

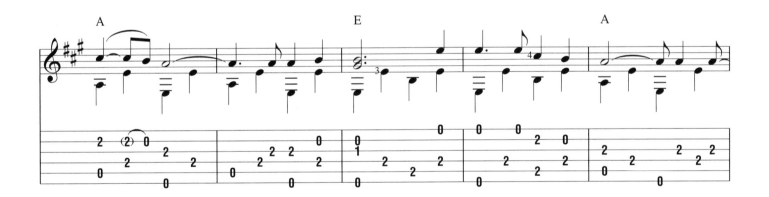

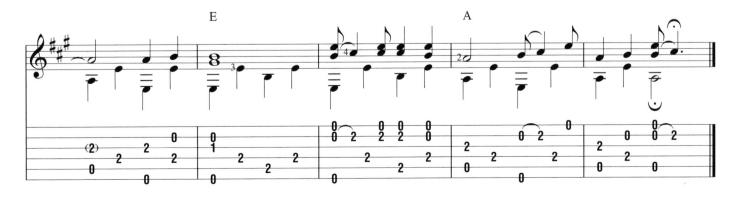

It's Mighty Dark to Travel

Words and Music by Bill Monroe

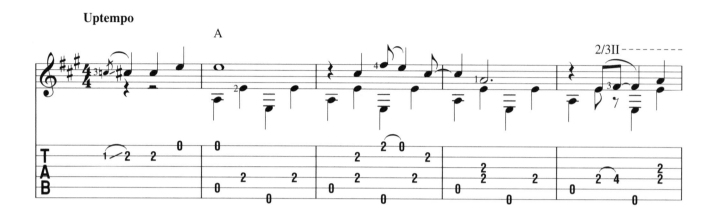

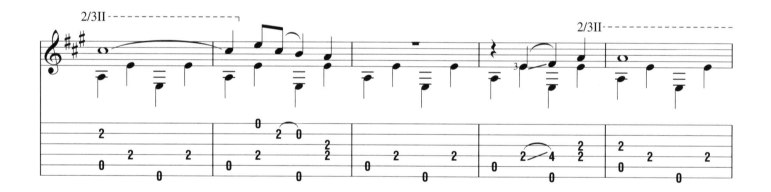

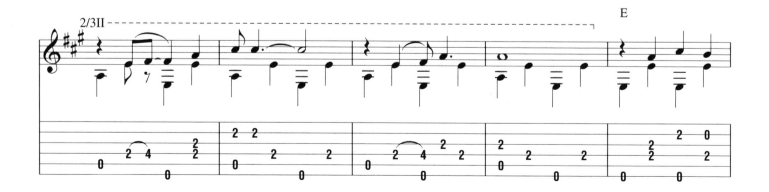

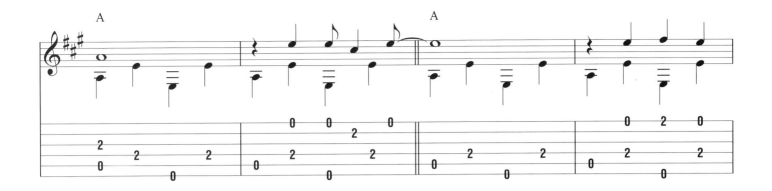

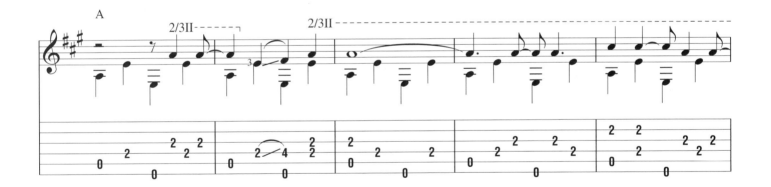

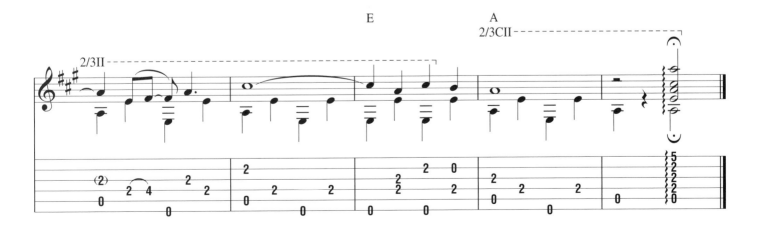

Let Me Love You One More Time

Words and Music by Ralph Stanley

*T = Thumb on 6th string

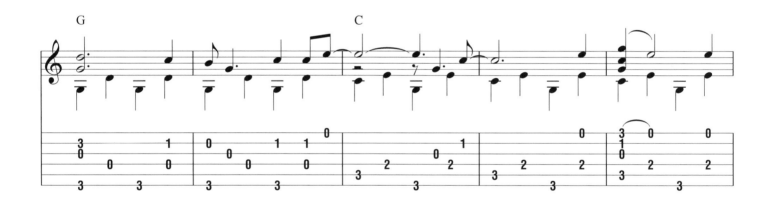

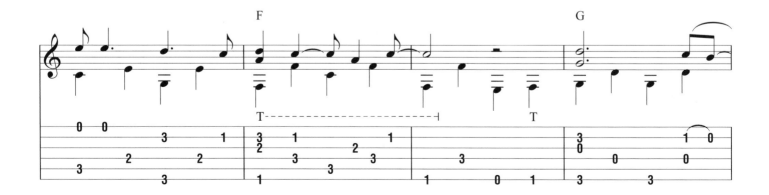

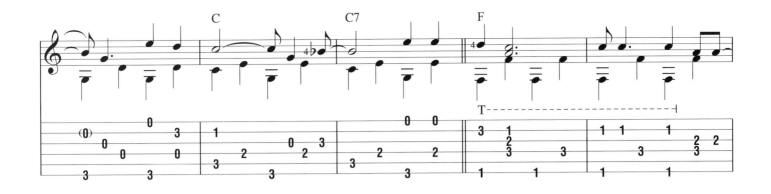

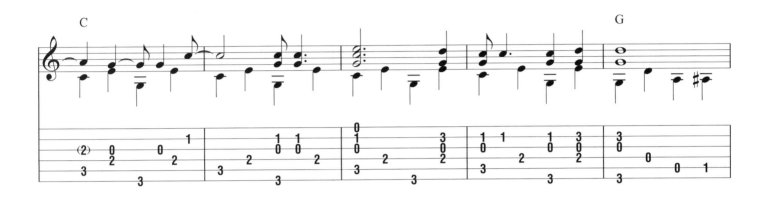

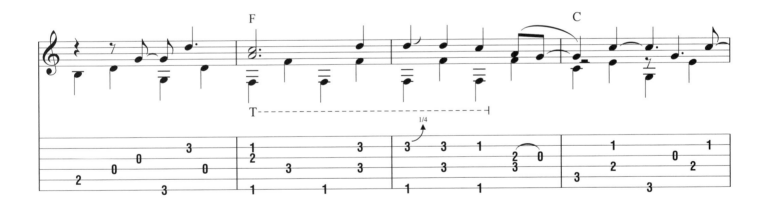

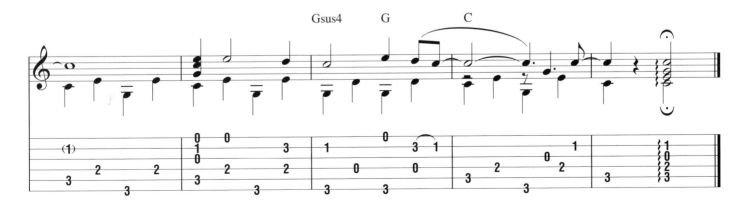

My Rose of Old Kentucky

Words and Music by Bill Monroe

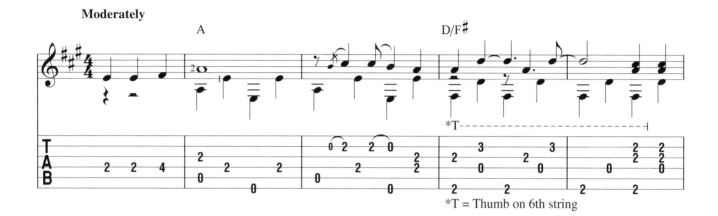

*T = Thumb on 6th string

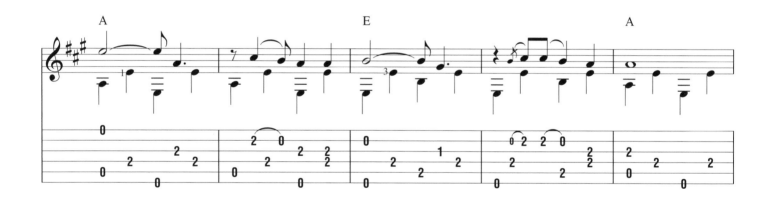

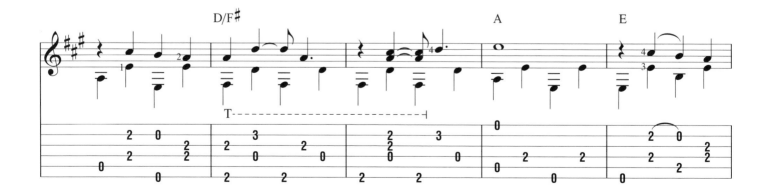

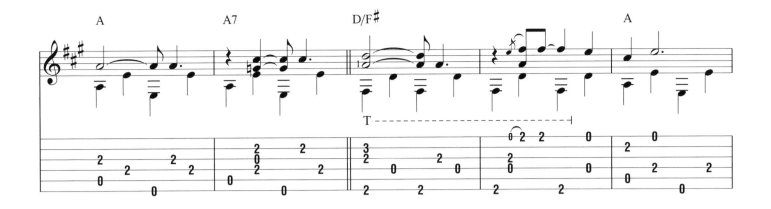

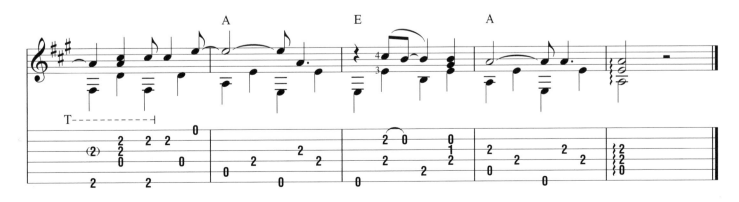

Uncle Pen

Words and Music by Bill Monroe

Drop D tuning:
(low to high) D-A-D-G-B-E

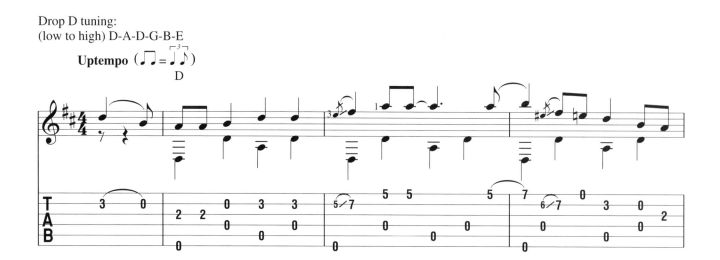

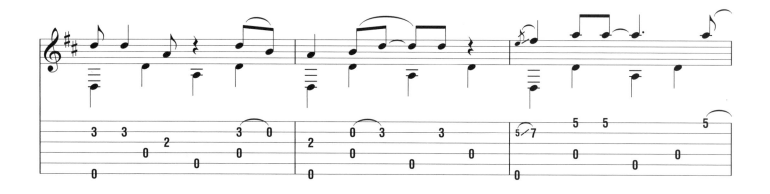

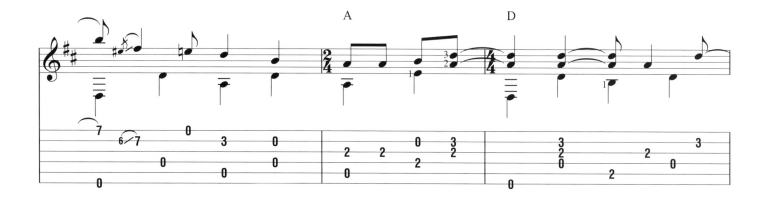

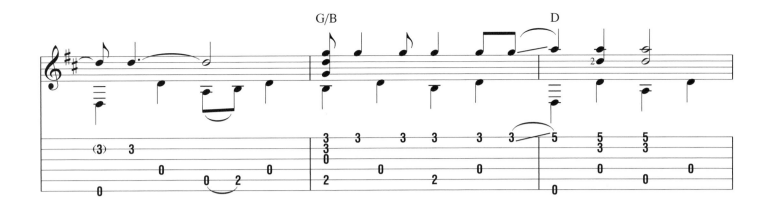

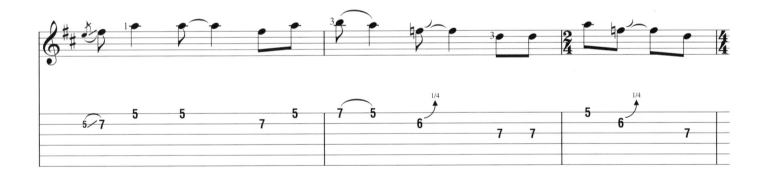

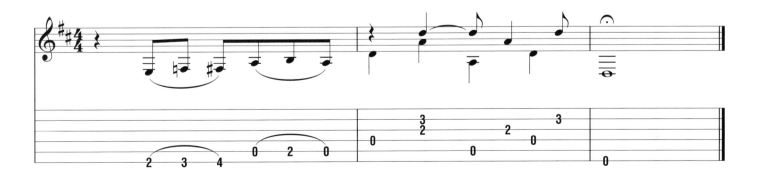

FINGERPICKING
GUITAR BOOKS

Hone your fingerpicking skills with these great songbooks featuring solo guitar arrangements in standard notation and tablature. The arrangements in these books are carefully written for intermediate-level guitarists. Each song combines melody and harmony in one superb guitar fingerpicking arrangement. Each book also includes an introduction to basic fingerstyle guitar.

FINGERPICKING ACOUSTIC
15 songs: Behind Blue Eyes • Best of My Love • Blowin' in the Wind • The Boxer • Dust in the Wind • Helplessly Hoping • Hey Jude • In My Life • Learning to Fly • Leaving on a Jet Plane • Tears in Heaven • Time in a Bottle • You've Got a Friend • and more.
00699614..$9.99

FINGERPICKING ACOUSTIC ROCK
15 songs: American Pie • Bridge over Troubled Water • Every Rose Has Its Thorn • Knockin' on Heaven's Door • Landslide • More Than Words • Norwegian Wood (This Bird Has Flown) • Suite: Judy Blue Eyes • Wanted Dead or Alive • and more.
00699764..$9.99

FINGERPICKING BACH
12 masterpieces from J.S. Bach: Air on the G String • Bourrée in E Minor • Jesu, Joy of Man's Desiring • Little Prelude No. 2 in C Major • Minuet in G • Prelude in C Major • Quia Respexit • Sheep May Safely Graze • and more.
00699793..$8.95

FINGERPICKING BALLADS
15 songs: Against All Odds • (Everything I Do) I Do It for You • Fields of Gold • Have I Told You Lately • It's All Coming Back to Me Now • Looks Like We Made It • Rainy Days and Mondays • Say You, Say Me • She's Got a Way • Your Song • and more.
00699717..$9.99

FINGERPICKING BEATLES
30 songs including: All You Need Is Love • And I Love Her • Can't Buy Me Love • Hey Jude • In My Life • Lady Madonna • Let It Be • Love Me Do • Michelle • Nowhere Man • Please Please Me • Something • Ticket to Ride • Yellow Submarine • Yesterday • and more.
00699049..$19.95

FINGERPICKING CHILDREN'S SONGS
15 songs: Any Dream Will Do • Do-Re-Mi • It's a Small World • Linus and Lucy • The Muppet Show Theme • Puff the Magic Dragon • The Rainbow Connection • Sesame Street Theme • Winnie the Pooh • Zip-A-Dee-Doo-Dah • and more.
00699712..$9.99

FINGERPICKING CHRISTMAS
20 classic carols: Away in a Manger • Deck the Hall • The First Noel • God Rest Ye, Merry Gentlemen • Hark! The Herald Angels Sing • It Came Upon the Midnight Clear • Jingle Bells • O Little Town of Bethlehem • Silent Night • What Child Is This • and more.
00699599..$8.95

FINGERPICKING CLASSICAL
15 songs: Ave Maria • Bourée in E Minor • Canon in D • Eine Kleine Nachtmusik • Für Elise • Habanera • Minuet in G Major (Bach) • Minuet in G Major (Beethoven) • New World Symphony • Pomp and Circumstance • and more.
00699620..$8.95

FOR MORE INFORMATION, SEE YOUR LOCAL MUSIC DEALER,
OR WRITE TO:

HAL•LEONARD®
CORPORATION
7777 W. BLUEMOUND RD. P.O. BOX 13819 MILWAUKEE, WI 53213

Visit Hal Leonard online at **www.halleonard.com**

FINGERPICKING COUNTRY
17 classic favorites: Always on My Mind • By the Time I Get to Phoenix • Could I Have This Dance • Crazy • Green Green Grass of Home • He Stopped Loving Her Today • I Walk the Line • King of the Road • Tennessee Waltz • You Are My Sunshine • and more.
00699687..$9.99

FINGERPICKING DISNEY
15 songs: The Bare Necessities • Beauty and the Beast • Can You Feel the Love Tonight • Colors of the Wind • Go the Distance • If I Didn't Have You • Look Through My Eyes • Reflection • Under the Sea • A Whole New World • You'll Be in My Heart • and more.
00699711..$9.95

FINGERPICKING HYMNS
15 songs: Amazing Grace • Beneath the Cross of Jesus • Come, Thou Fount of Every Blessing • For the Beauty of the Earth • I've Got Peace like a River • Jacob's Ladder • A Mighty Fortress Is Our God • Rock of Ages • and more.
00699688..$8.95

FINGERPICKING ANDREW LLOYD WEBBER
14 songs: All I Ask of You • Don't Cry for Me Argentina • Memory • The Music of the Night • With One Look • more.
00699839..$9.99

FINGERPICKING MOZART
15 of Mozart's timeless compositions: Ave Verum • Eine Kleine Nachtmusik • Laudate Dominum • Minuet in G Major, K. 1 • Piano Concerto No. 21 in C Major • Piano Sonata in A • Piano Sonata in C • Rondo in C Major • and more.
00699794..$8.95

FINGERPICKING POP
Includes 15 songs: Can You Feel the Love Tonight • Don't Know Why • Endless Love • Imagine • Let It Be • My Cherie Amour • My Heart Will Go On • Piano Man • Stand by Me • We've Only Just Begun • Wonderful Tonight • and more.
00699615..$9.99

FINGERPICKING PRAISE
15 songs: Above All • Breathe • Draw Me Close • Great Is the Lord • He Is Exalted • Jesus, Name Above All Names • Oh Lord, You're Beautiful • Open the Eyes of My Heart • Shine, Jesus, Shine • Shout to the Lord • You Are My King • and more.
00699714..$8.95

FINGERPICKING ROCK
15 songs: Abracadabra • Brown Eyed Girl • Crocodile Rock • Free Bird • The House of the Rising Sun • I Want You to Want Me • Livin' on a Prayer • Maggie May • Rhiannon • Still the Same • When the Children Cry • and more.
00699716..$9.99

FINGERPICKING STANDARDS
17 fantastic songs: Can't Help Falling in Love • Fly Me to the Moon • Georgia on My Mind • I Just Called to Say I Love You • Just the Way You Are • Misty • Moon River • Unchained Melody • What a Wonderful World • When I Fall in Love • Yesterday • and more.
00699613..$9.99

FINGERPICKING WEDDING
15 tunes for the big day: Beautiful in My Eyes • Don't Know Much • Endless Love • Grow Old with Me • In My Life • The Lord's Prayer • This Is the Day (A Wedding Song) • We've Only Just Begun • Wedding Processional • You and I • and more.
00699637..$9.99

FINGERPICKING YULETIDE
16 holiday favorites: Blue Christmas • The Christmas Song • Frosty the Snow Man • A Holly Jolly Christmas • I'll Be Home for Christmas • Jingle-Bell Rock • Let It Snow! Let It Snow! Let It Snow! • Merry Christmas, Darling • Rudolph the Red-Nosed Reindeer • and more.
00699654..$9.99

Prices, contents and availability subject to change without notice.